Mak
time

Learn how to manage your time and make more time for yourself

Kate Keenan

Published by Pocket Manager Books
1 Queena Square
Bath BA1 2HA

www.pocketmanagerbooks.com

Print ISBN: 978-1-909179-52-3
eBook ISBN: 978-1-909179-65-3
Pdf ISBN: 978-1-909179-79-0

A CIP catalogue record for this book is available from the
British Library.

Previously published as The Management Guide to Making Time
by Oval Books, 1995, 1998.

Original series editor – Anne Tauté, Oval Books
Editor – Catriona Tulloch Scott
Project manager – Clare Christian, The Book Guru
Book and cover re-design – Philip Jansseune, Walker Jansseune
Image enhancement – Matt Holland, MiH Design
Author photograph – Marko Dutka, Studio Marko

*Cover: Imprecise time is the resort of those who could do better at
managing it.*

Contents

This book is dedicated to
those who would like to manage better
but are too busy to begin.

To download your **FREE** Workbook
which accompanies
Make time

please visit:

**www.pocketmanagerbooks.com/books/
make-time**

Make time

Time is a finite commodity. To literally 'make time' is not possible; however, you can certainly get more done in the time you have available. Once time has been spent, it can never be recovered. When it has gone, you have even less time to do what you want to do. But with a little dexterity and a fair following wind, you can certainly get more done in the time that you have at your disposal.

Everyone has the same amount of time available. Most people admit that they do not have enough time, yet some of them manage to get so much more done than others. Understanding why this is the case plays a vital part in helping you to manage your time more productively.

To save time, you need to spend a little time up front. Unless you take some time to work out what you are trying to achieve both on a long-term and daily basis, you will only waste more time.

This book looks at what you can do, if not to make more time then, at least, to make the most of it.

1 The need to make time

Nobody likes to think that they waste time. But not only is it extremely easy to do this, half the time you may not even realise that this is what you are doing. Here are some examples:

- Going over the same ground twice because you have forgotten something the first time round.
- Only achieving half of what you had planned for the day and not knowing why.
- Wondering what on earth ever happened to the best part of the day.
- Seeing your 'to do' list of things getting longer.
- Seeing your 'pending' tray getting larger or your electronic inbox growing exponentially.
- Not being able to find that essential piece of paper when you need it.
- Spending time looking for something in the wrong place because you cannot remember where you originally put it.

You may recognise some of these symptoms which chiefly seem to relate to poor self-organisation. In the short-term, most people can get away with not being too well organised. But in the longer-term, this may end up as a serious problem.

What is getting in the way

Working out how to make effective use of your time requires you to examine some of the things which may be getting in the way. This may be a bit difficult, as no one likes to think they waste their time or other people's.

Much of the secret of managing time has to do with how well organised you are. If you have scant regard for administrative procedures, you will probably find the idea of being organised rather a nuisance.

But in fact, being well organised will help you save large amounts of time – always provided you do not become so obsessed with devising systems to save time, that you end up wasting it.

Find the cause

To manage time well, you need to be really honest with yourself. Ask yourself these questions and answer them as truthfully as you can.

- What do I do that need not be done at all?
- What do I do that could and should be done by someone else?
- What do I do that is taking longer than it should?
- What do I do that possibly wastes other people's time?

Your answers to these four questions provide you with the cornerstone for making the most of your time.

Things that need not be done at all

This is a very common way of wasting time. Not only are you producing things that you do not need, you could also be producing things which no-one else needs either. You may recognise some of the following scenarios:

- You are still doing something because it has always been done. Do you actually know what happens to this work? Is the output genuinely useful, or does it simply get filed or stored and never looked at again?
- You still keep several sets of books into which transactions are laboriously entered – just in case.
- You are still running a manual system after it has all been computerised simply because you do not trust the new system.

All these activities are inevitably wasting time, and also do not contribute very much to your overall output.

Things that could and should be done by someone else

Doing things which could and should be done by someone else is tempting, especially when it is work which you are, or have been, good at. But if you do not delegate certain tasks you will have less time to devote to managing. It often seems quicker to do something yourself than to spend time delegating it, and even when you have delegated a task you may find it difficult to resist the temptation to keep stepping in at the slightest hint of a difficulty. But if you do, you face further time-wasting situations because:

- You will be spending your time doing something which someone else is meant to do.
- People will learn very quickly that if they have a problem you will sort it for them.
- You will not doing what you should be doing.

What is more, many will resent your help, while others will cease to bother trying in the first place. In the meantime, your own efficiency is at risk and you may end up having to delegate tasks for which you are responsible to those who cannot do them well enough, and who then need you to help them once more. So it becomes a vicious circle.

Things that take longer than they should

If you find that you are not as efficient as you would like to be, this may be because:

- You are not very well organised and cannot find all the relevant things you require to complete a job.
- You find a task demanding because you have not taken the time to inform yourself properly what is needed.
- You rush into action before you have worked out exactly what it is you need to do.
- You are trying to do everything yourself.

If any of these sound familiar, try reflecting on what is involved in the various tasks. This will help you to determine more realistic time-frames for completing the tasks you need to do as well as help you avoid overrunning your schedule.

Things that waste other people's time
Nobody likes to admit that they might possibly be causing other people to waste time. Most people will say they never have enough time of their own, so how can they possibly waste other people's? But think about some of the following situations:

- Having second thoughts after people have already done a great deal of work.
- Forgetting to pass on new information so people are still working on old, out-of-date information.
- Asking people to see you about something and then neglecting to have the relevant papers or material to hand, and then you waste time looking for them.
- Holding impromptu meetings that have no agenda, so people do not know what the meeting is about and cannot prepare themselves.
- Allowing interruptions so that discussion lasts much longer than it should and is less effective.
- Keeping punctual people waiting, with or without an explanation, because you are running late.

If you plead guilty to any of these, think how much time in total may be being lost through your actions. For example, if your lack of preparation for a meeting of 10 people means that it lasts 25 minutes longer than necessary, you have wasted a total of 250 minutes which is more than half a working day.

Plausible excuses

There are plenty of plausible reasons for not being able to get things done on time. But as everyone has the same amount of time at their disposal, it must be the way individuals manage time which makes the difference. In fact, there is no such thing as not having enough time to do something. One can always make time. What is usually lacking is the motivation.

So if you find yourself saying, *'I haven't got time'* when asked to do something, you need to understand that what you are really saying is that you don't want to find time because you don't really want to do this. For instance, no matter how busy you are, who wouldn't find the time to attend a champagne reception in Paris, all expenses paid?

You may fail to get things done on time because:

- The task does not appear to be worth making much of an effort for.
- Inactivity does not seem to have any serious immediate penalties.

- There are more interesting things to do.
- You haven't given yourself a deadline.

If you fool yourself into believing your own excuses for not doing things, you will never get down to doing something about managing your time better. Probably in your heart of hearts, you know that you will have to face up to your own shortcomings, if you are to use your time better. Be honest with yourself and identify the real reasons why things either do not get done at all or do not get finished on time.

It is possible that a task is taking a long time because you find it difficult, perhaps because you do not possess the necessary skills. You may not be able to do all that you are required to do, so you end up falling behind.

If you are avoiding an important task in the hope it will go away, it tends not to and usually ultimately ends up as a self-imposed crisis – and crises are prize methods of wasting time. The answer is to spend some time learning how to become competent in that task and so avoid a crisis.

Ask yourself how satisfied you are with the way you use the time you have available. It may be that you are reasonably effective but feel you could do better. Very probably the things you are not getting done on time are those you may not want to do or tend to find more difficult to tackle.

A useful strategy here is to make a record of how you are currently spending your time. This gives you an objective benchmark against which to measure your progress in managing time.

Decide to make more time for yourself

Your attitude will directly reflect whether you want to be positive in managing your time or whether you want to use being restricted time as an excuse for being ineffective.

It requires the will on your part to put things right and make the most of the time you have available. Once you have made the decision to do better at making more time for yourself, the rest is comparatively easy.

Questions to ask yourself

To assess whether you are managing your time as effectively as you could, think about your answers to the following questions:

- Do I find it difficult to say what I have done during a day?

- Do I find meeting deadlines can be a problem?

- Do I ever do things which really do not need to be done?

- Do I tend to take over other people's work for them?

- Do I tend to take longer than I should on certain tasks?

- Do I find it difficult to get to appointments on time?

- Do I often forget what I was going to do?

If you have answered 'Yes' to many of these questions, your ability to manage time may require some attention.

You will be doing better if…

- You spend a little time thinking about how you use your time.

- You can identify some of the things you are doing that waste your time.

- You can recognise which reasons are really excuses for not completing something, or for not doing something at all.

- You can clearly indicate your main achievements at the end of each day.

- You have a positive attitude towards wanting to manage your time

2 Plan your tasks

Churchill said that if you want a thing done, you should give it to a busy person. Busy people seem better at controlling time than others. They seem to be able to cram more things into their day than anyone else. Because these people are busy, they will always find a way to fit what is required into their schedule. The reasons for this are often because these people:

- Have a sense of urgency about getting things done.
- Take deadlines seriously and do not like missing them.
- Have developed the skills they require to make sure they achieve things on time.
- Are fully aware of what they are responsible for producing.

By developing and adopting these personal qualities, you will greatly enhance your ability to use your time.

Know what you are responsible for

In business, every job has a job title and, by implication, this job description that outlines those areas for which you are personally responsible.

It is by being fully aware of what you are there to do that you can identify what you should be doing and compare this with what you are actually doing.

If you do not have a job description, it is a good idea to construct one for yourself. Identify the main responsibilities of your job. Make a list of the tasks you need to accomplish to do your work effectively. Think carefully about what the real scope of your job is, and how it contributes to the overall effectiveness of your business or profession.

You may find you do certain things which are not central to ensuring effective performance in your work. They may be fun and enjoyable, but you need to recognise they are not the core tasks for which you are being paid.

The first step in making more time is to clearly understand what your responsibilities are: what exactly you are there for. Once you have understood this, it is far easier to establish your goals and identify where your priorities lie.

Set yourself goals

Setting and achieving goals plays a major part in managing time. If you do not know what you are aiming for, you will not know where to start, nor be able to recognise when you've got there.

Knowing what is important and needs to be done puts you in control of events rather than events being in control of you. Goals are useful because they enable you to:

● Focus your attention on where you are going.

- Plan what to do within a given time-frame.
- Help others understand what is happening and how they fit into the scheme.

Having an objective prevents you from wasting time. To set goals effectively you need to:

- Work out what you want to achieve.
- Discuss your thoughts with someone else.
- Write down what you resolve to do, and stick to it.

By keeping your goals constantly in mind, you will be more able to focus on what you need to achieve in the time you have available.

Identify your priorities

It will help you achieve your goals if you identify your priorities. To do this, look at your workload as a whole and decide which activities are top priority. These can be categorised under four headings:

- **Essential tasks** These are the ones which if you did not perform, you would not fulfil your role effectively.
- **Tasks which you should perform** These should be done once the top priority tasks have been carried out.
- **Tasks you would like to do in the fullness of time** These are usually the things that never get done.

- **Tasks that have a low priority** These are usually easy and fun. These are often the ones you find most attractive and usually get done first.

List the tasks facing you under these four headings. Look at your list and assign time to what you need to do, what you should do, and what you would like to do.

This helps you to eliminate activities which you like doing, but which are not essential. It also allows you to do a non-essential, but enjoyable, task from time to time in the full knowledge that it is not high priority, but that you are doing it as a reward for doing other longer, more complex tasks.

Once you have identified where your priorities lie, try not to stick so rigidly to them that you cannot change course if circumstances should dictate. If you can be flexible in your approach, this will help you manage the inevitable contingencies which arise, no matter how well you schedule your time. Situations can change dramatically and cause your current priorities to become irrelevant. Sticking to them in these circumstances can only waste time.

However, should a priority activity disappear, for instance, a meeting is cancelled, watch out that you do not simply fritter that allocated time away. Use the energy you had activated for that completed task to tackle another of the tasks on your list.

Urgency and importance

Understanding the difference between what is urgent and what is important plays a significant part in making time.

Things that are urgent are those which are pressing in their need for attention, even if they are trivial; for example, sorting out car parking arrangements prior to visitors attending a meeting. Things that are important require careful consideration and usually need extra time to think about; for example, your business plan for the next quarter.

Urgent things have a habit of looking important because of their time constraints. They require quick reactions, but they should not take up too much of your time. You may sometimes have to put off something which is urgent to attend to something which is important.

There may also be occasions when putting off important things in order to do something more immediately interesting is fine, provided you do it on purpose. If you want to take time to do something of this sort, work out how to recoup the time, then you can enjoy doing it without guilt or remorse.

You will, of course, encounter some things that prove to be both urgent and important. When both these conditions apply, the matter requires your fullest attention. There is no question of doing something more appealing first. The penalty will be that you run out of time.

Types of task

Think about the nature of the things you do. Consider how much of your time is taken up with executive activities and how much time is spent performing day-to-day tasks specific to your business or profession.

Managing tasks means engaging in key activities, such as planning, organising, directing and controlling, and requires you to:

- Think ahead to ensure you have all you need to run things efficiently and effectively.
- Have the right people and the right materials in the right place at the right time.
- Let people know what they need to do and the standard they should achieve, and if necessary, coach them on how to do it.
- Make sure that relevant people know what is going on and what they have to do to ensure that things go well.

Look at your list of priorities. If you are not performing any of the above key functions to any great degree, analyse what it is that you are in fact doing and how it fits in with your key responsibilities.

You may find that you are letting others off-load tasks which they find difficult on to you because you are better at them than they are. Or it could be that you are held up owing to a lack of the right systems or equipment.

Most of all, you may not have realised that it is your competence in carrying out executive tasks which makes a real contribution to saving time.

No time to lose

By identifying your responsibilities, knowing what your goals are, putting your tasks in order of priority, and being able to distinguish between those tasks that are urgent and those that are important, you will find it easier to plan how to use your time more effectively.

If this all sounds a bit exacting and time-consuming, it is worth considering the story of the Chinese Emperor. He indicated to his estate manager that he would like an avenue of cedar trees to lead up to his palace.

The manager objected. *'It will take 300 years for this project to come to fruition,'* he pointed out. *'Well,'* said the Emperor, *'you haven't got a minute to lose.'*

Questions to ask yourself

Think about how you go about planning your time and answer the following questions:

- Do I fully understand what are my responsibilities and what are not my responsibilities?

- Am I clear about my goals and what I want to achieve?

- Have I identified where my priorities lie?

- Do I know what I should achieve today, if I do nothing else?

- Can I distinguish between what is important and what is urgent?

- Am I working on the right type of tasks to make more effective use of my time?

You will be doing better if...

- You can identify your essential tasks.

- You identify your goals.

- You get your important work done within a pre-determined timescale.

- You understand the need to be flexible when priorities change unexpectedly.

- You distinguish between urgent and important work.

- You carry out the right sort of executive tasks which assist you in managing your time better.

- You resolve to start planning your time right away.

3 Schedule your time

Organising your time would be made a great deal simpler if other people did not always want things from you so that you never seem to get your own work finished.

Whatever the day brings or the world outside demands, you need to develop a range of strategies to help you outwit such contingencies and make the best use of your time.

Deal with deadlines

Parkinson's Law states that all work expands to fill the time available for its completion. This is why having deadlines is so important. Without them, very little tends to happen within a sensible time-frame.

Once deadlines have been determined, you can set your own deadlines within them, like a box within a box. This prevents you from allowing a task to fill all the time you have available.

Give yourself a time limit on various activities. Set your watch, mobile phone or computer clock, or keep an alarm clock handy, to alert you that your time is up. You will be surprised how this concentrates the mind and how much you get done in the time you have allocated.

What is more, as you get used to working within set time limits, you will find yourself completing work in less and less time.

Tackle large tasks

Large tasks can appear daunting. Because of this, you may find that this can lead to inactivity simply because you do not know where to start. For example, if it fell to you to arrange the relocation of the entire office, it is important you are not intimidated by the complexity and magnitude of the task.

The trick is to confront any large job by treating it as you would treat eating a watermelon – by cutting it into manageable chunks. Once you have done this, work out a schedule for dealing with the chunks and tackle one bit at a time. The large task will now appear to be magically possible and you can plot your progress against your schedule.

Set aside undisturbed time

Certain things need your undivided attention and you should set aside uninterrupted time to do these things. Many people achieve this by finding another, quieter place to work, but there are several other ways to prevent interruptions by organising 'exclusive' time:

- **Decide on times when you are available** Also designate times when you are not to be disturbed, and tell people which are which.
- **Set your voicemail to take messages when you are there** Do this for an hour or two as this gives you space to get

essential work done. You can deal with the messages one after the other at a chosen time.

- **Install a 'white board' in your bathroom** Possibly with waterproof pens, so you can write and plan in peace.
- **Keep a notebook bedside your bed** It is extraordinary how many times an important thought occurs when you are at your most relaxed.

Ensuring that you have a period of undisturbed time allows you to focus and use your time fruitfully.

Make the most of meetings

How often have you said on emerging from a meeting: *'That meeting was a complete waste of time'*? For example, regular weekly meetings may have become superfluous without anyone noticing this. But meetings need not waste time. When you take charge of any meeting, make sure you know the answers to these questions:

- *'Why does anyone need to be meeting at all? Wouldn't an e-mail or telephone call do just as well?'*
- *'Who should attend and why?'*
- *'What precise topics will be discussed?'*
- *'What do I want to achieve from the meeting?'*

Every person attending should know these things in advance if the meeting is to be productive.

If a good deal of your time is taken up by attending meetings, make sure you know:

- The purpose of the meeting.
- Your specific role in it.
- The actions you need to take after it.

If you do not know these three things, question why you are going to the meeting in the first place; and whether you need to be present the whole time, or whether you can simply make your own contribution and learn the rest from the Minutes.

There are some circumstances when a face-to-face meeting may be more appropriate. For example.

- When you have never met before.
- When you need to get a feel for how others are getting on with each other, or judge a particular person's capabilities.
- When a social atmosphere is helpful to the outcome.
- When the situation is so involved that evaluating body language will be as important as verbal communication (if not more so).

Otherwise, it might be much more beneficial to telephone, e-mail, or set up a teleconferencing call, all of which are readily available and relatively easy to mange.

Use journey time effectively

Making a journey is often related to attending meetings and has equal potential in the time-wasting stakes. It's also a good policy always to question the purpose of making any journey. If you travel on business, or you are faced with a journey, make the most of this 'dead' time, particularly if you are travelling by train.

- Take your laptop or personal organiser with you to do some work or answer your e-mails.
- Clear out your briefcase, making sure you take your 'litter' back to the office shredder, in a plastic bag if necessary.
- Dig out receipts from your pockets, wallet and briefcase and collate them for expenses claims.
- Listen to a management tape, a talking book, or perhaps start a language course.
- Think about strategy, formulate plans and make notes for future reference.
- Read a book that you have been meaning to read for ages.
- Listen to a tape on some uplifting subject or bone up on some business topic you need to know about.

By planning your journey time positively, you can use this personal space for doing essential preparation and catching up, as well as engaging in some serious thinking.

Allocate your time

If you can schedule time for your work in a way which allows you to get things done, you will be more able to meet your deadlines. You will have set aside the time to do what you need to do and, as a result, you will find that you have made time to do all sorts of things you never had time for previously.

By deliberately working to self-imposed time limits you will prevent time allocated for one thing over-running and leaking into the time allocated to something else. You will also feel more confident that you are better at making time work for you, rather than being overtaken by it. This gives you the assurance that you are in charge of your working life and that you can achieve the endless numbers of things required of you on time.

Questions to ask yourself

Think about how you schedule your time and answer these questions:

- Am I meeting my deadlines?

- Have I broken down large tasks into their component parts?

- Have I got a method of setting aside uninterrupted time so as to get important things completed?

- Am I getting the best out of the meetings I attend?

- Are all my journeys necessary?

- Do I plan how I will use the time I have available if I make long-distance journeys?

- Am I scheduling my activities efficiently and making best use of the time I have at my disposal?

You will be doing better if...

- You meet external deadlines by imposing internal ones of your own.

- You use a number of positive ways to enjoy uninterrupted time.

- You tackle large tasks by breaking them down into manageable chunks.

- You get more out of the meetings you choose to attend.

- You plan what work to do when you make a journey.

- You complete your activities within a given time.

4 Save time

Saving time is easier than you think. It is all about getting yourself organised. There are a number of excellent and practical ways of doing this, most of which are relatively simple and do not demand too much time to implement.

Make lists

Many people think they are able to do several things at the same time. They are usually mistaken, and end up either doing things rather badly or not completing them at all. The secret is to do things in an orderly way by making lists to remind yourself what you should be doing.

Making lists is a key activity in getting organised. Your lists should reflect your priorities and contain details of what you intend to do. Writing things down is often halfway to getting them done. This gives you focus as well as something tangible to follow.

Here are some examples of the types of lists which will help quite significantly in the process of controlling time:

● **Make a list of things you must achieve today** If the list exceeds six things, you are highly unlikely to do them all. If an item stays on your list for more than three days, ask yourself why this is so. It is likely that the situation will now be at crisis point, will have resolved itself, or was never worth doing in the first place.

- **Put your items into a sensible working order** This helps you to move easily from one task to the next. By doing this, you will feel that you are more in control of events, rather than the other way round.
- **Write down what you want to do when you leave your desk** If you get side-tracked, you can easily forget what you were going for in the first place and may return to your desk without having accomplished even one of the things you intended to do.

Many people resist the formality of writing simple things down, but memory can let you down. Research indicates that seven items (plus or minus two) are the maximum number of things you can remember easily. But it seems that if you are interrupted when you are trying to remember even a few items in your mind, the number that can be recalled becomes even less. So write down what has to be done. By doing so:

- You do not forget anything important.
- You do not have to make a second journey or telephone call to complete your tasks.
- You can tick off the things you have completed, giving you a real sense of achievement.

Using lists to guide your activities enables you to concentrate better on what you need to do. You are less likely to be side-tracked because you have a reminder of what you have to do.

Handle paperwork

There are several pitfalls which can prevent you from being properly organised. An untidy desk, briefcase, cupboard or car may indicate that you are somewhat unsure of how to manage yourself or your paperwork. Rather than throw anything out you keep it all. The way to deal with paperwork is to handle it once, and once only. Each time a piece of paper comes your way take action in one of the following four ways:

- File it.
- Act upon it.
- Pass it on.
- Bin it.

The last is the one that causes people the most problems because they are reluctant to take the decision to throw a piece of paper away. It is probable that the use of the bin as an organisational tool is given less importance than it should be.

The squirrel instinct is endemic and not one to be encouraged if you want to manage your time more effectively. If the paper is of no use to you, be ruthless, get rid of it. If you really cannot bring yourself to do so, then have a tray marked 'Fog Bound', 'Deep Litter', or whatever, for things which you cannot make up your mind about. After a few months, take the bottom third and, without looking at it, throw it away. If it has not become urgent by the time you do this, surely it cannot be all that important.

Keep personal records

Knowing what has occurred on a day-to-day basis is important, especially as other people's perceptions may not always be quite the same as yours.

To make sure that at least you know you are right, it's sensible to record things as they occur. So you need to:

- **Keep a dedicated note-book** In this you write down everything from daily reminders to the resolutions of the board meeting. Have it with you at all times.
- **Keep paper and pens by the telephone** It is amazing how many people do not. You find this out just as you are about to give them details of something, when they say, *'Just a minute, I need to find a pen.'*
- **Make sure your contacts list is up-to-date** This should include important names, along with e-mail addresses and their current telephone numbers, both landline and mobile.
- **Log important mail and telephone calls** Note these in your working diary, so that you know when things happened and when you responded.

Your personal records play a vital part in helping you doing business. By keeping them updated you will become more efficient and save time in the long-run.

Find things easily

If you have a good retrieval system, you will find things quite quickly. If your system is poor or non-existent, it is worth spending time organising one.

Make sure you keep it simple. Few people need a complicated cross-reference system. It rarely helps you to find items any faster and probably requires more time to file in the first place. Sort out a system to suit your own needs and make sure you know how it works so that you can find things instantly when you need them.

Some simple filing systems, which might seem a little old-fashioned but work very efficiently, might include:

- Well-labelled box files for major projects.
- A tray marked 'Immediate' for each day's six tasks.
- Individual pocket folders for various topics, kept in alphabetical order.
- A concertina wallet for keeping documents in chronological order.
- A set of index cards for keeping comprehensive customer records, filed alphabetically, or by product.
- A stack of envelopes labelled by month in which you put your receipts.

- A brightly-coloured folder or box file marked 'VIP' where you put all your important bits and pieces. Being brightly coloured means that you never lose track of it.

Knowing exactly where you keep pieces of paper is crucial in controlling your time. But be sure that whatever is meant to go into a file is actually put there. Much of this is common sense, but it is often the small disciplines which help a great deal more in managing your time well than all the technological personal time systems and fancy wall-charts in the world.

Take shortcuts

Getting behind is a universal problem. Desperate measures are needed on occasions when there is simply no time to function as you usually would. For instance, you could:

- **Use e-mail to get back quickly to people** Be brief, to the point and, above all, polite.
- **Use your wastepaper basket** Don't waste time filing something you don't need to keep. If in doubt, have a 'Just in case' folder, but make sure you clear it out at regular intervals.
- **Set a timer for your telephone calls** This is particularly useful when the person you are calling is inclined to waffle. The audible 'ping' when the time is up provides an obvious signal to bring the conversation to a close.

No doubt you will have devised many other shortcut-type responses. The key is to communicate speedily and save time rather than using the more formal channels. Shortcuts give you more time to get on with what you need to be doing.

Become more organised

There are many things which can get in the way of being able to manage your time efficiently. It is important to make sure that your lack of personal organisation is not one of them.

Keeping tidy makes it easier to find things quickly and stops you wasting time by having to look for things in unlikely places. Responding instantly by using emergency tactics means you will be able to make time for most things when a real log-jam has occurred.

When you are personally organised, you stay in control of what you should and can control.

Questions to ask yourself

Think about how you organise yourself and answer the following questions:

- Do things stay on my 'to do' list for several days?

- Do I forget to do things simply because I did not write them down?

- Do I tend to temporarily lose important memos, letters and documents?

- Do I forget appointments or day-to-day routine activities?

- Do I handle paperwork several times before actioning it?

- Is it hard to find things when I need them in a hurry?

- Do I always seem to be trying to do too many things at the same time?

You will be doing better if...

- You make lists of things you need to do.

- You handle your paperwork only once.

- You use the wastepaper basket with confidence.

- You find important things in seconds rather than minutes.

- You have a workable retrieval system that suits your needs.

- You keep records of events.

- You keep abreast of the deluge by taking short cuts.

- You feel considerably more confident that you have things under control.

- You have not mislaid anything for some time.

5 Work efficiently with others

Other people are an essential part of business, but they can be great time-wasters. Working efficiently with people plays an important part in managing your time effectively.

When you are very busy it is tempting to say, *'I'll do it myself; that way I'll make sure it gets done and I'll know it's all right.'* This is fine for a little while, when you are up against unexpectedly tight schedules. But in the long run, if you do not spend some time teaching someone else to do the task you will have burdened yourself with an unwanted extra, simply because there is no-one else who can do it. If a task takes an hour of your time every week and if teaching someone else to do it will only take a total of two to three hours, you could save yourself around fifty hours in the course of the year.

Delegate work

Passing tasks on to others allows you more time for yourself. However, in the 'leaner and fitter' business environment, finding someone to pass the tasks to may not be so easy.

People often think that delegating is simply about handing out work willy-nilly and hoping that someone will do it properly. But there are some points which need to be observed if you are to ensure that tasks get done correctly and on time. To delegate well, you need to:

- **Choose someone who is willing** It is important to have a willing and competent volunteer. Remember they also should be able to do what needs to be done.
- **Discuss with the person concerned** Indicate precisely what you would like done and, if necessary, exactly how you would like the work carried out. Let the person know the timescale for the task and indicate how often you would like to be given a progress report. Make it clear you are available for consultation when necessary.
- **Allocate a priority to the work being delegated** It is important to make sure that this can be fitted in with other work that the person has to do.
- **Assign authority for the task** It is essential to ensure that the person responsible for the task can actually carry it out. And if the work requires liaison with others, especially with senior people, make sure you 'smooth the path' for the person concerned. Above all, you need to avoid introducing anyone who is unprepared and unsupported into situations that may be fraught with problems such as those associated with 'company politics'.
- **Show that you care about the outcome** You want successful completion of the task. If others know that you care about it being completed successfully and on time, they will also care about achieving this.
- **Regularly review progress** Discuss any problems being encountered while carrying out the work, especially if you are developing a person's skills.

If you do not make it clear what is required and why, the task will be brought back to you to do all over again yourself. You may also have irretrievably upset an individual you are delegating to, since he or she will not only have failed to complete the task but will also have wasted their time.

There are two other important things to remember when handing over tasks. You need to:

- **Pass out the good as well as the bad** Delegating efficiently means passing out the good things as well as the not-so-good things. It will soon be noticed if you only delegate the dreary tasks and keep all the attractive ones yourself. If this is happening, you cannot be surprised if someone is reluctant to take on work from you or does not complete it on time.
- **Know what is involved** No work should ever be delegated which you find difficult to do yourself. If you have problems, how on earth will other people do any better than you? This is when you should be going to someone more expert to seek assistance, not leaving someone who is not competent to struggle on, and ultimately be defeated and demoralised by the task.

Delegation is an important skill to master in the quest to make more time for yourself. Initially it involves using some time. But if you can reserve time and hand over a task in an encouraging way, not only will you ultimately free up more time for yourself, but also others will also be motivated to ensure they make best use of their time. A double benefit.

Work productively together

Being aware of other people's time will help you to ensure that they value yours. Here are some ideas on how to use time wisely when working on joint efforts:

- **Ensure you pass on relevant information** This needs to be done at the time you receive it. If others get this information too late they will have wasted their time working to the original instructions. Or they will waste your time interrupting you to ask questions.
- **Remember to tell others** If you have a brilliant idea which causes you to change your mind, let people know immediately. If you do not, they will continue to carry out previously agreed activities which may not now be relevant, and end up wasting valuable time.
- **Agree deadlines** Those involved need to know how you arrived at the timing of the deadline. Say, *'We need to get this done by next Tuesday, and the reason for this is because...'* You will find people more likely to get things done on time when they understand why.
- **When needing to work late** It is essential to make sure the task is urgent and not something that could be done

next day. Otherwise you will have not only caused them to give up their personal time but they will be less willing to take on urgent work next time you ask.

Working conjointly is a great way to stretch the time available and achieve remarkable results. If you can treat other people's time as if it was as precious as yours, you will be well on the way to maximising your output.

Communicate effectively

Communicating is basically about making sure other people have understood the information you have for them or what you would like them to do It is also about ensuring that you have understood the instructions and information given to you.

When you communicate well, you also save yourself time, as people understand what is needed the first time around.

Consider how you give information or instructions to others, and make sure that you:

● **Use clear, everyday words when giving instructions**
Make sure that there is no ambiguity in what you say. This increases the chances of things being right first time. It is extraordinary how few people will take the time to do something right the first time, yet will somehow find the time to re-do it.

- **Check people write down important information** When you are on the telephone, ask them to repeat it back to you to ensure they have got the message.
- **Help people to leave a coherent message** Ask people, when recording a message, to give not only their name and number but also the time and day that they called. It is surprising how many calls are overtaken by events which often make messages redundant.

Conversely, you can help others to make better use of your time by confirming the information and instructions you are given. To do this, you should:

- **Verify that you have understood what is required** Always ask questions to clarify points of detail to ensure you know what needs to be done.
- **Write down important information** This is essential when talking on the telephone. Also read it back to ensure its accuracy.
- **Say who you are** Let people know the day and time that you called, what your message relates to and a contact telephone number, when you leave a message on voicemail,

These disciplines are part and parcel of communicating effectively. They are well worth the time you spend on them as they prevent the time-wasting aggravation of having to unravel mis-understandings and mis-information. When you communicate effectively, this contributes considerably to making the best possible use of your time.

When work is delegated to you

Working with others involves managing their time as well as your own. If other people are disorganised, they can waste your time. So you have to help them to make better use of your time and theirs by discussing with them:

- Why the work has to be done.
- What is wanted, precisely.
- When the work is required.
- What form the work should take.

Knowing why the work is needed can give valuable clues as to what has to be done. If the work is for internal use, a rough draft may be enough. Being able to focus on the end-receiver prevents you from providing unnecessary information and thus wasting time. Knowing in what form it is required is even better. Producing a five-page report when a verbal briefing would have done is clearly a waste of time.

Work out if what you have been asked to do fits in with your priorities. This way, you can make a sensible assessment as to whether what is requested can be fitted in without detracting from your own activities. If you do not find out, you can be laden with work not of your own making, and may be unable to complete any of it satisfactorily. You may be seen as a busy person, but also as one who is unable to get anything done on time.

Share time

Helping others to help you make better use of your time is an essential part of managing your time well.

Delegating work can save you time if you make sure people know what they are doing, but you need to communicate properly and spend a little time ensuring that they are quite clear about what is required of them. Equally, when you take on work you need to clarify exactly what it is that you are expected to do. More often than not others may neglect to inform you sufficiently about what is required and you could waste valuable time doing what you think is needed rather than what actually is.

It is alarming how much time is wasted repeating tasks unnecessarily. So it is never a waste of time to check that you have fully understood what is needed. Making certain of the facts means that everyone can make better use of their time.

Questions to ask yourself

Assess how well you are making the best use of your time and other people's by answering the following questions:

- Do I delegate enough?

- Do I follow the 'rules' when passing out work?

- Do I always indicate that I care about the results of the tasks I delegate?

- Do I make sure that if I require urgent work from someone, it does have to be done immediately and not tomorrow?

- Do I give clear instructions about what has to be done and why?

- Do I always make sure that I have fully understood what is required of me?

- Do I take the time to check what exactly needs to be done, so that the task will not have to be done all over again?

You will be doing better if...

- You delegate certain tasks instead of doing them all yourself.

- You follow the guidelines when delegating.

- You pass out interesting tasks and routine tasks in equal proportions.

- You prevent other people from wasting your time and theirs.

- You communicate clearly and you check that you are properly understood.

- You verify what is required of you before you go ahead and do it.

- You cannot think of anything you have done recently which has wasted other people's time.

6 Make time for yourself

Getting your work done and accommodating others takes up most of your time, so it is easy to find yourself last in the line for attention.

When you examine the ways you use time in your personal life, you may see how you can put yourself at the head of the queue.

Revise your personal habits

Think of everything you do from the time you wake up the morning. Work out how your personal routine (or maybe lack of it) could be losing you time. Think of what you might have to do to change your routine to make it more time-efficient. Here are a few examples to consider:

- **Tidy up** If you are somewhat untidy, it might be sensible to find a quick way of tidying up your surroundings so that you do not have to waste time finding things.
- **Save time** If you are having to go some distance for certain services, maybe you could find a company that collects and delivers and save yourself some vital time.
- **Change your journey to work** If you are still using the same route you took to work on your first day, you may not have explored other options. There are probably several other ways which may turn out to be quicker or better on certain days. You won't know until you try.

By taking an objective look at your personal habits, you will probably find that there is quite a range of simple changes you can make which will gain you more time.

Take leisure time

It is really important to make sure you schedule your leisure time, otherwise you will never get any. This is particularly critical if you work for yourself. It may seem a bit extreme to schedule time off, but if work expands to fill the time, it is easy to see how you can miss out.

You may already be caught in a well-known trap. On the one hand, you feel that you should be working whenever you take a little time off. On the other hand, when you are working long hours with no let-up, you may tend to feel quite resentful that while others seem to be leading full social lives, you never seem to be able to.

The way out of the conundrum is simple. Give yourself permission to take time off. There are a number of excellent ways to do this:

- **Block out your holiday period in advance** This means that you cannot be coerced into working instead. You simply say you are busy that week.
- **Make a contract with yourself to take off specific periods of time** For instance, Saturday is your day off, but Sunday afternoons are a good time for you to catch up and plan for the next week.

- **Find something that is a complete contrast from work** If you can find a little time in each day to do this, you will restore you spirits and gain more energy to keep going.

Making time for leisure is just as important to your efficiency as work is. It allows you to refresh your mental faculties and your physical performance.

It also means that your family and friends see you from time to time. Support from them enables you to keep things in perspective. Similarly they may need support from you, and if you never make time for them, a time may come when they may not be there for you.

It is vital to your well-being, and therefore to your working ability, to make time for pleasure and personal relationships. It makes sense to remind yourself that there is not much point in allowing work to take up all your time if you have no opportunity to enjoy the rewards which come from it.

Put yourself in the equation

Your private life is not so separate from your working life as you may think. If you can take time to revise some of your personal habits, it could help you to find the time to do more.

It is vital you build time into your busy schedule to re-energise yourself and so enjoy the benefits that your efforts in managing time better will undoubtedly bring.

Questions to ask yourself

Think about how you can make more time for yourself.
Answer the following questions.

- Are there any personal habits I can change to make the use of my time more efficient and more enjoyable?

- Are there any things I do simply because I always have?

- Do I spend enough time on myself?

- Do I have specific time set aside for activities that have nothing whatsoever to do with work?

- Am I taking time to enjoy the fruits of my labours?

You will be doing better if...

- You revise some of your personal habits to prevent yourself from wasting time.

- You manage your time, rather than letting time manage you.

- You do not let work take you over, but actively schedule time off from work for your own pursuits and recharge your batteries.

- You are no longer feeling guilty that you should be working when you are not.

- You are able to place yourself if not actually at the head of the queue for attention, then very near it.

Check your progress

If you find that making better use of your time is proving to be a bit harder than you thought, check how you are tackling these key areas.

Analyse your use of time

If you are constantly running out of time, it could be that you have not yet fully analysed the use you make of your time. When you know how you use your time, you set up an important method of how you can measure the improvements you have made.

Know your priorities

If you are not absolutely sure of your priorities, you may find you have been doing time-consuming things which do not contribute very much to your overall effectiveness. When you make sure you know where your priorities lie and stick to them, you tend to get a lot more done.

Get organised

If you cannot find things and tend to be personally disorganised, it may be that you need to change some of your habits. Changing a routine is not easy, but if you take some time to examine the balance between your work and home life, you will inevitably find a number of ways you can save time.

Plan your time

If you have not developed robust strategies for using the time you have available to your advantage, you could be finding that you are overwhelmed by events and never catch up with your workload. For example, you did not think to take appropriate documents to read when travelling by train. It is vital to plan what you want to achieve in any given situation, or you will find that you are constantly wasting precious time.

Delegate

If you are still doing everything yourself, perhaps you are not using other people's talents to best effect. Others can be of considerable help in allowing you to use your time better. If you take a little time to think about what you could delegate and do it properly, you can not only help other people to develop their own skills but you can also save yourself time in the future.

Make time for yourself

If you find that work keeps getting on top of you, and you lack energy to cope, you need to consider whether you are taking enough time to unwind from work. Scheduling leisure time for yourself to regain energy allows you to work hard and play hard.

Reap the benefits

You have to want to make better use of your time. If you take managing time seriously and try to put into practice some of the ideas that have been suggested, you should find yourself less hard-pressed and with more time at your disposal. When this happens, you will be able to put the time gained to good use as you will be able to:

- Plan more thoroughly.
- Create new ideas or start new projects.
- Develop your skills.
- Take care of yourself.
- Foster your personal interests.

Managing your time better can usually be achieved by thinking about the possible courses of action open to you, rather than rushing directly into action.

If you are saying to yourself, *'This is all very well, but it can't be as simple as that,'* you would be right. Trying to manage your time is not easy. Some days things will go well for you and you will feel you have achieved a great deal. On other days, events will overcome you and all your best-laid plans will fall apart. You must not give up, saying that it is all too difficult, but determine to try again the next day. Remember the Chinese Emperor's cedars and start right now.

Glossary

Here are some definitions in relation to Make time.

Attitudes
  Embedded views that can influence the way you get things done.

Competence
  Ability to do something efficiently and effectively and thus make full use of your time.

Crises
  Time-wasting happenings which could have been prevented, but which have now reached panic proportions.

Deadlines
  Fixed points that limit the amount of time available to waste.

Delegating
  Passing on the right things to the right people.

Diary
  The simplest tool which has ever been devised for personal organisation.

Effectiveness
  Ensuring that the right things get done.

Efficiency
  Ensuring that things get done in the right way. You can be very efficient, but also totally ineffective.

Excuses
Very poor, if not downright pathetic, reasons for not doing something

Important
Something that matters; not the same thing as 'Urgent'.

Organising
Ensuring that you make maximum use of resources when time is at a premium.

Priorities
What you must do, rather than what you would like to do.

Responsibilities
Issues for which you are entirely accountable, usually too many.

Retrieval system
Ingenious method of making sure you find something quickly the next time you need it.

Squirrel instinct
Hiding your nuts so well that you can't find them again.

Urgent
Something that needs doing within a tight time-frame, not necessarily important.

Wasted time
Opportunities which will never recur.

Further reading

Make time provides you with an overview of the basic skills you need to develop to help you find more time to do those things you really want to do.

Below are some other resources which you might find useful when developing and enhancing your skills further in the area of time management.

Mike Clayton (2010)
> **Brilliant Time Management**: *What the Most Productive People Know, Do and Say* (Brilliant Business), Harlow: Pearson Education Limited.

Mark Forster (2006)
> **Do it Tomorrow** *and Other Secrets of Time Management*, London: Hodder & Stoughton.

Julie Morgenstern (2004)
> **Time Management**, New York: Owl Books.

Fergus O'Connell (2013)
> **The Power of Doing Less**: *Why Time Management Courses Don't Work and How to Spend Your Precious Life on the Things That Really Matter*, Chichester: Capstone Publishing Ltd.

About the author

Kate Keenan, CPsychol, AFBPsS, BA, BSc, MSc, MPhil, has over 20 years experience as a chartered psychologist and is expert in the areas of occupational and organisational psychology. Kate specialises in promoting psychological wellbeing in the workplace. She has worked extensively with corporate and independent businesses, devising strategic management programmes that enable them to identify and resolve managerial issues – from personnel selection and individual assessment to team building and attitude surveys.

She also works as a mentor and coach, offering a series of practical and transformative evidence-based strategies designed to help people make the most of their opportunities, both business and personal. In particular, she helps entrepreneurs and business owners maximise their prime asset – themselves.

Kate has a post-graduate qualification in Mental Health Studies from Kings College, London and currently lives in Bath.

In terms of being able to **make time** for herself, she says:

'I have been a tireless advocate of making more time. I have learned the hard way that it is always later than you think. I now enjoy helping others to manage their time considerably better sooner that I learned to do so.'

Pocket Manager Books

'Especially for people who neither have the time nor the inclination for ploughing through the normal tomes...'

Personal wellbeing

- Manage yourself
- Make time
- Assert yourself
- Handle stress

Essential business skills

- Plan
- Solve problems
- Communicate
- Negotiate
- Run meetings

Effective leadership

- Manage
- Recruit
- Motivate
- Delegate
- Understand people

More information about these books available at…
www.pocketmanagerbooks.com

To download your FREE Workbook
which accompanies **Make time**

please visit:

www.pocketmanagerbooks.com/books/
make-time

An environmentally friendly book printed and bound in England by www.printondemand-worldw

PEFC Certified

This product is
from sustainably
managed forests
and controlled
sources

www.pefc.org

PEFC
PEFC/16-33-415

MIX
Paper from
responsible source:

FSC
www.fsc.org

FSC® C004959

s book is made entirely of sustainable materials; FSC paper for the cover and PEFC paper for the

Reprint of # - C0 - 177/111/4 - PB - Lamination Matt - Printed on 06-Mar-17 12:29